F. W. H. (Frederic William Henry) Myers

Saint Paul

F. W. H. (Frederic William Henry) Myers

Saint Paul

ISBN/EAN: 9783742856791

Manufactured in Europe, USA, Canada, Australia, Japa

Cover: Foto ©Lupo / pixelio.de

Manufactured and distributed by brebook publishing software
(www.brebook.com)

F. W. H. (Frederic William Henry) Myers

Saint Paul

Cambridge:

PRINTED BY C. J. CLAY, M.A.

AT THE UNIVERSITY PRESS.

BY

FREDERIC W. H. MYERS.

𝔏𝔬𝔫𝔡𝔬𝔫 𝔞𝔫𝔡 ℭ𝔞𝔪𝔟𝔯𝔦𝔡𝔤𝔢:

MACMILLAN AND CO.

1867.

DEDICATED

TO

J. E. B.

ᾗ καὶ τὴν ἐμὴν ψυχὴν ὀφείλω.

SAINT PAUL.

"There is neither Jew nor Greek, there is neither bond nor free, there
is neither male nor female: for ye are all one in Christ Jesus."

CHRIST! I am Christ's! and let the name suffice you,
    ay, for me too He greatly hath sufficed;
lo with no winning words I would entice you,
    Paul has no honour and no friend but Christ.

Yes, without cheer of sister or of daughter,
    yes, without stay of father or of son,
lone on the land and homeless on the water
    pass I in patience till the work be done.

Yet not in solitude if Christ anear me
  waketh him workers for the great employ,
oh not in solitude, if souls that hear me
  catch from my joyaunce the surprise of joy.

Hearts I have won of sister or of brother
  quick on the earth or hidden in the sod,
lo every heart awaiteth me, another
  friend in the blameless family of God.

What was their sweet desire and subtle yearning,
  lovers and ladies whom their song enrols?
Faint to the flame which in my breast is burning,
  less than the love with which I ache for souls.

Oh ye are kind, I shall abide and teach you,
  ye will not fail as men have failed before,
seek me and leave, ashamed when I beseech you,
  ever less loving as I love the more.

Yet it was well, and Thou hast said in season
  'As is the Master shall the servant be':
Let me not subtly slide into the treason,
  seeking an honour which they gave not Thee:

never at even, pillowed on a pleasure,
  sleep with the wings of aspiration furled,
hide the last mite of the forbidden treasure,
  keep for my joys a world within the world,—

nay but much rather let me late returning
  bruised of my brethren, wounded from within,
stoop with sad countenance and blushes burning,
  bitter with weariness and sick with sin:—

so to thy presence get me and reveal it,

  nothing ashamed of tears upon thy feet,

show the sore wound and beg thine hand to heal it,

  pour thee the bitter, pray thee for the sweet.

Then with a ripple and a radiance thro' me

  rise and be manifest, o Morning Star!

Flow on my soul, thou Spirit, and renew me,

  fill with Thyself, and let the rest be far.

Safe to the hidden house of thine abiding

  carry the weak knees and the heart that faints,

shield from the scorn and cover from the chiding,

  give the world joy, but patience to the saints.

Saints, did I say? with your remembered faces,

 dear men and women, whom I sought and slew!

Ah when we mingle in the heavenly places

 how will I weep to Stephen and to you!

Oh for the strain that rang to our reviling

 still, when the bruised limbs sank upon the sod,

oh for the eyes that looked their last in smiling,

 last on this world here, but their first on God!

Let no man think that sudden in a minute

    all is accomplished and the work is done;—

Though with thine earliest dawn thou shouldst begin it

    scarce were it ended in thy setting sun.

Oh the regret, the struggle and the failing!

    oh the days desolate and useless years!

vows in the night, so fierce and unavailing!

    stings of my shame and passion of my tears!

How have I seen in Araby Orion,

    seen without seeing, till he set again,

known the night-noise and thunder of the lion,

    silence and sounds of the prodigious plain!

How have I knelt with arms of my aspiring
　　lifted all night in irresponsive air,
dazed and amazed with overmuch desiring,
　　blank with the utter agony of prayer!

'What,' ye will say, 'and thou who at Damascus
　　sawest the splendour, answeredst the voice,
so hast thou suffered and canst dare to ask us,
　　Paul of the Romans, bidding us rejoice?'

Shame on the flame so dying to an ember!
　　shame on the reed so lightly overset!
Yes, I have seen him, can I not remember?
　　yes, I have known him, and shall Paul forget?

I, even I who from the fleshly prison
　　caught, (I believe it but I dare not say,)
rose to the mid light of the Lord arisen,
　　woke to the waking rapture of the day,—

ah they are shut, the ears of my divining,
  sealed are the eyes that should have seen Him then:
look what a beam from the Beloved shining!
  look what a night of treasonable men!

What was their tale of some one on a summit,
  looking, I think, upon the endless sea,—
one with a fate, and sworn to overcome it,
  one who was fettered and who should be free?

Round him a robe, for shaming and for searing,
  ate with empoisonment and stung with fire,
he thro' it all was to his lord uprearing
  desperate patience of a brave desire.

Ay and for me there shot from the beginning
  pulses of passion broken with my breath;
oh thou poor soul, enwrapped in such a sinning,
  bound in the shameful body of thy death!

Well, let me sin, but not with my consenting,

well, let me die, but willing to be whole:

never, o Christ,—so stay me from relenting,—

shall there be truce betwixt my flesh and soul.

Oft shall that flesh imperil and outweary
  soul that would stay it in the straiter scope,
oft shall the chill day and the even dreary
  force on my heart the frenzy of a hope :—

lo as some ship, outworn and overladen,
  strains for the harbour where her sails are furled ;—
lo as some innocent and eager maiden
  leans o'er the wistful limit of the world,

dreams of the glow and glory of the distance,
  wonderful wooing and the grace of tears,
dreams with what eyes and what a sweet insistance
  lovers are waiting in the hidden years :—

lo as some venturer, from his stars receiving

  promise and presage of sublime emprise,

wears evermore the seal of his believing

  deep in the dark of solitary eyes,

yea to the end, in palace or in prison,

  fashions his fancies of the realm to be,

fallen from the height or from the deeps arisen,

  ringed with the rocks and sundered of the sea :—

so even I, and with a heart more burning,

  so even I, and with a hope more sweet,

groan for the hour, o Christ! of thy returning,

  faint for the flaming of thine advent feet.

What can we do, o'er whom the unbeholden
  hangs in a night with which we cannot cope?
what but look sunward, and with faces golden
  speak to each other softly of a hope?

Can it be true, the grace He is declaring?
  oh let us trust Him, for his words are fair!
Man, what is this, and why art thou despairing?
  God shall forgive thee all but thy despair.

Truly He cannot, after such assurance,
  truly He cannot and He shall not fail;
nay, they are known, the hours of thine endurance,
  daily thy tears are added to the tale:

never a sigh of passion or of pity,

   never a wail for weakness or for wrong,

has not its archive in the angels' city,

   finds not its echo in the endless song.

Not as one blind and deaf to our beseeching,

   neither forgetful that we are but dust,

not as from heavens too high for our up-reaching,

   coldly sublime, intolerably just :—

nay but thou knewest us, Lord Christ, thou knowest,

   well thou rememberest our feeble frame,

thou canst conceive our highest and our lowest,

   pulses of nobleness and aches of shame.

Therefore have pity!—not that we accuse thee,

   curse thee and die and charge thee with our woe :

not thro' thy fault, o Holy One, we lose thee,

   nay, but our own,—yet hast Thou made us so!

Then tho' our foul and limitless transgression
   grows with our growing, with our breath began,
raise thou the arms of endless intercession,
   Jesus, divinest when thou most art man!

Also I ask, but ever from the praying

   shrinks my soul backward, eager and afraid,

Point me the sum and shame of· my betraying,

   show me, o Love, thy wounds that I have made !

Yes, thou forgivest, but with all forgiving

   canst not renew mine innocence again:

Make thou, o Christ, a dying of my living,

   purge from the sin but never from the pain!

So shall all speech of now and of· to-morrow,

   all He hath shown me or shall show me yet,

spring from an infinite and tender sorrow,

   burst from a burning passion of regret:

standing afar I summon you anigh him,

   yes, to the multitudes I shout and say,

'This is my King! I preach and I deny him,

   Christ! whom I crucify anew to-day.'

See, when a fireship in mid ocean blazes

    lone on the battlements a swimmer stands,

looks for a help, and findeth not, and raises

    high for a moment melancholy hands;

then the sad ship, to her own funeral flaring,

    holds him no longer in her arms, for he

simple and strong and desolate and daring

    leaps to the great embraces of the sea.

So when around me for my soul's affrighting,

    madly red-litten of the woe within,

faces of men and deeds of their delighting

    stare in a lurid cruelty of sin,

thus as I weary me and long and languish,

   nowise availing from that pain to part,—

desperate tides of the whole great world's anguish

   forced thro' the channels of a single heart,—

then let me feel how infinite around me

   floats the eternal peace that is to be,

rush from the demons, for my King has found me,

   leap from the universe and plunge in Thee!

Thou with strong prayer and very much entreating
   willest be asked, and thou shalt answer then,
show the hid heart beneath creation beating,
   smile with kind eyes and be a man with men.

Were it not thus, o King of my salvation,
   many would curse to thee and I for one,
fling thee thy bliss and snatch at thy damnation,
   scorn and abhor the shining of the sun,

ring with a reckless shivering of laughter
   wroth at the woe which thou hast seen so long,
question if any recompense hereafter
   waits to atone the intolerable wrong:

3

is there not wrong too bitter for atoning?

what are these desperate and hideous years?

hast Thou not heard Thy whole creation groaning,

sighs of the bondsmen, and a woman's tears?

Yes, and to her, the beautiful and lowly,

Mary a maiden, separate from men,

camest thou nigh and didst possess her wholly,

close to thy saints, but thou wast closer then.

Once and for ever didst thou show thy chosen,

once and for ever magnify thy choice;—

Scorched in love's fire or with his freezing frozen,

lift up your hearts, ye humble, and rejoice!

Not to the rich He came and to the ruling,

(men full of meat, whom wholly He abhors,)

not to the fools grown insolent in fooling

most, when the lost are dying at the doors;

nay but to her who with a sweet thanksgiving
took in tranquillity what God might bring,
blessed Him and waited, and within her living
felt the arousal of a Holy Thing.

Ay for her infinite and endless honour
found the Almighty in this flesh a tomb,
pouring with power the Holy Ghost upon her,
nothing disdainful of the Virgin's womb.

East the forefront of habitations holy
　　gleamed to Engedi, shone to Eneglaim;
softly thereout and from thereunder slowly
　　wandered the waters, and delayed, and came.

Then the great stream, which having seen he showeth,
　　hid from the wise but manifest to him,
flowed and arose, as when Euphrates floweth,
　　rose from the ankles till a man might swim.

Even with so soft a surge and an increasing,
　　drunk of the sand and thwarted of the clod,
stilled and astir and checked and never-ceasing
　　spreadeth the great wave of the grace of God;

bears to the marishes and bitter places
  healing for hurt and for their poisons balm,
isle after isle in infinite embraces
  floods and enfolds and fringes with the palm.

Ay and afar to realms and to recesses
  seen in a storm, discovered in a dream,
fields which no folk nor any power possesses,
  oceans ungirdled of the ocean-stream :—

yes or if loose and free, as some are telling,
  (little I know it and I little care,)
this my poor lodge, my transitory dwelling,
  swings in the bright deep of the endless air,—

round it and round his prophets shall proclaim him,
  springing thenceforth and hurrying therethro',—
each to the next the generations name him,
  honour unendingly and know anew.

Great were his fate who on the earth should linger,
   sleep for an age and stir himself again,
watching Thy terrible and fiery finger
   shrivel the falsehood from the souls of men.

Oh that thy steps among the stars would quicken !
   oh that thine ears would hear when we are dumb !
Many the hearts from which the hope shall sicken,
   many shall faint before thy kingdom come.

Lo, for the dawn, (and wherefore wouldst thou screen it?)
   lo with what eyes, how eager and alone,
seers for the sight have spent themselves, nor seen it,
   kings for the knowledge, and they have not known.

Times of that ignorance with eyes that slumbered
   seeing He saw not, till the days that are,
now, many multitudes whom none hath numbered,
   seek him and find him, for he is not far.

Ay and ere now, a triumph and a token,
   flown o'er the severance of the sundering deep,
came there who called, and with the message spoken
   followed the winging of the ways of sleep.

Ay and ere now above the shining city
   full of all knowledge and a God unknown
stood I and spake, and passion of my pity
   drew Him from heaven and showed him to his own.

Heard ye of her who faint beneath the burthen
  strained to the cross and in its shadow fell?
Love for a love, the angels' for the earthen,—
  Lord and Redeemer, surely it was well!

She as one wild, whom very stripes enharden,
  leapt many times from torture of a dream,
shrank by the loathly olives of the garden,
  groves of a teacher, and Ilissus' stream:

then to their temple Damaris would clamber,
  high where an idol till the dawn was done
bright in a light and eminent in amber
  caught the serene surprises of the sun.

Thence the strong soul, which never power can pinion,
  sprang with a wail into the empty air,
thence the wide eyes upon a hushed dominion
  , looked in a fierce astonishment of prayer:

looked to Hymettus and the purple heather,

    looked to Peiræus and the purple sea,

blending of waters and of winds together,

    winds that were wild and waters that were free.

So from the soft air, infinite and pearly,

    breathed a desire with which she could not cope,

could not, methinks, so eager and so early,

    chant to her loveliness the dirge of hope :

could not have done with weeping and with laughter

    leaving men angry and sweet love unknown,

could not go forth upon a blank hereafter

    weak and a woman, aimless and alone.

Therefore with set face and with smiling bitter

    took she the anguish, carried it apart,—

ah, to what friend to speak it ? it were fitter

    thrust in the aching hollows of her heart.

Then I preached Christ: and when she heard the
    story,—
  oh, is such triumph possible to men?
Never, my King, had I beheld Thy glory,
  never had known Thine excellence till then.

Thou from on high perceivest it were **better**
  all men and women should on earth be free :
laws that blaspheme and tyrannies that fetter
  snap and evanish at the touch of Thee.

Where is the soul with which thou wilt not tarry,
  raise from her nothingness and love her long?
His, shall I say? who to the end must carry
  hid in his body the extremest wrong?

Nay, but for him a birth and a baptizing
  came in the fair flow of the stranger stream,
whence he arose as when a seer arising
  wears in his eyes the wonder of a dream.

Gone was the saint, nor staying for another,

    home thro' the wilderness he read and ran,

bought and adopted, and in Christ a brother,

    claimed and completed, and in Christ a man.

Once for the least of children of Manasses

    God had a mission and a deed to do,

wherefore the welcome that all speech surpasses

    called him and hailed him greater than he knew;

asked him no more, but took him as he found him,

    filled him with valour, slung him with a sword,

bad him go on until the tribes around him

    mingled his name with naming of the Lord.

Also of John a calling and a crying

    rang in Bethabara till strength was spent,

cared not for counsel, stayed not for replying,

    John had one message for the world, Repent.

John, than which man a grander or a greater

    not till this day has been of woman born,

John like some iron peak by the Creator

    fired with the red glow of the rushing morn.

This when the sun shall rise and overcome it

    stands in his shining desolate and bare,

yet not the less the inexorable summit

    flamed him his signal to the happier air.

This is His will: He takes and He refuses,

    finds him ambassadors whom men deny,

wise ones nor mighty for his saints He chooses,

    no, such as John or Gideon or I.

He as He wills shall solder and shall sunder,

    slay in a day and quicken in an hour,

tune him a chorus from the Sons of Thunder,

    forge and transform my passion into power.

Ay, for this Paul, a scorn and a reviling,

   weak as you know him and the wretch you see,—

Even in these eyes shall ye behold His smiling,

   strength in infirmities and Christ in me.

Often for me between the shade and splendour
  Ceos and Tenedos at dawn were grey,
welling of waves, disconsolate and tender,
  sighed on the shore and waited for the day.

Then till the bridegroom from the east advancing
  smote him a waterway and flushed the lawn
God with sweet strength, with terror, and with trancing,
  spake in the purple mystery of dawn.

Oh what a speech, and greater than our learning!
  scarcely remembrance can the joy renew;
what were they then, the sights of our discerning,
  sorrows we suffer, and the deeds we do?

Lo every one of them was sunk and swallowed,

morsels and motes in the prodigious sea;

far was the call, and farther as I followed

grew there a silence round the Lord and me.

Oh could I tell ye surely would believe it!

oh could I only say what I have seen!

how should I tell or how can ye receive it,

how, till He bringeth you where I have been?

Therefore, o Lord, I will not fail nor falter,

nay but I ask it, nay but I desire,

Lay on my lips thine embers of the altar,

seal with the sting and furnish with the fire;

give me a voice, a cry and a complaining,—

oh let my sound be stormy in their ears!

throat that would shout but cannot stay for straining,

eyes that would weep but cannot wait for tears.

Quick in a moment, infinite for ever,

    send an arousal better than I pray,

give me a grace upon the faint endeavour,

    souls for my hire and Pentecost to-day!

Lo as some bard on isles of the Aegean
  lovely and eager when the earth was young,
burning to hurl his heart into a paean,
  praise of the hero from whose loins he sprung;—

he, I suppose, with such a care to carry,
  wandered disconsolate and waited long,
smiting his breast, wherein the notes would tarry,
  .chiding the slumber of the seed of song:

then in the sudden glory of a minute
  airy and excellent the proëm came,
rending his bosom, for a god was in it,
  waking the seed, for it had burst in flame.

So even I athirst for His inspiring,
 I who have talked with Him forget again,
yes, many days with sobs and with desiring,
 offer to God a patience and a pain;

Then thro' the mid complaint of my confession,
 then thro' the pang and passion of my prayer,
leaps with a start the shock of his possession,
 thrills me and touches, and the Lord is there.

Lo if some pen should write upon your rafter
 mene and mene in the folds of flame,
think you could any memories thereafter
 wholly retrace the couplet as it came?

Lo if some strange intelligible thunder
 sang to the earth the secret of a star,
scarce could ye catch, for terror and for wonder,
 shreds of the story that was pealed so far:—

Scarcely I catch the words of His revealing,
    hardly I hear Him, dimly understand,
only the Power that is within me pealing
    lives on my lips and beckons to my hand.

Whoso has felt the Spirit of the Highest
    cannot confound nor doubt Him nor deny:
yea with one voice, o world, tho' thou deniest,
    Stand thou on that side, for on this am I.

Rather the earth shall doubt when her retrieving
    pours in the rain and rushes from the sod,
rather than he for whom the great conceiving
    stirs in his soul to quicken into God.

Ay, tho' thou then shouldst strike him from his glory
    blind and tormented, maddened and alone,
even on the cross would he maintain his story,
    yes, and in hell would whisper, I have known.

God, who at sundry times in manners many
   spake to the fathers and is speaking still,
eager to find if ever or if any
   souls will obey and hearken to His will:—

who that one moment has the least descried Him,
   dimly and faintly, hidden and afar,
doth not despise all excellence beside Him,
   pleasures and powers that are not and that are:—

ay amid all men bear himself thereafter

smit with a solemn and a sweet surprise,

dumb to their scorn and turning on their laughter

only the dominance of earnest eyes?—

God, who whatever frenzy of our fretting

vexes sad life to spoil and to destroy,

lendeth an hour for peace and for forgetting,

setteth in pain the jewel of his joy:—

I am persuaded that no thing shall sunder

us from the love that saveth us from sin,

lift it or lose hereover or hereunder,

pluck it hereout or strangle it herein.—

Gentle and faithful, tyrannous and tender,

ye that have known Him, is He sweet to know?

softly He touches, for the reed is slender,

wisely enkindles, for the flame is low.—

God, who when Enos on the earth was holy
    saved him from death and Noe from the sea,
planned Him a purpose that should ripen slowly,
    found in Chaldaea the elect Chaldee,—

God, who for sowing of the seed thereafter
    called him from Charran, summoned him from Ur,
gave to his wife a weeping and a laughter,
    light to the nations and a son for her,—

God, who in Israel's bondage and bewailing
    heard them and granted them their heart's desire,
clave them the deep with power and with prevailing,
    gloomed in the cloud and glowed into the fire,

fed them with manna, furnished with a fountain,
    followed with waves the raising of the rod,
drew them and drave, till Moses on the mountain
    died of the kisses of the lips of God,—

God, who was not in earth when it was shaken,

    could not be found in fury of the flame,

then to his seer, the faithful and forsaken,

    softly was manifest and spake by name,

showed him a remnant barred from the betrayal,

    close in his Carmel, where the caves are dim,

so many knees that had not bent to Baal,

    so many mouths that had not kissed him,

God, who to glean the vineyard of his choosing

    sent them evangelists till day was done,

bore with the churls, their wrath and their refusing,

    gave at the last the glory of His Son:—

Lo as in Eden when the days were seven

    Pison thro' Havilah that softly ran

bare on his breast the changes of the heaven,

    felt on his shores the silence of a man:

silence, for Adam when the day departed
　　left him in twilight with his charge to keep
careless and confident and single-hearted
　　trusted in God and turned himself to sleep:

then in the midnight stirring in his slumber
　　opened his vision on the heights and saw
new without name or ordinance or number,
　　set for a marvel, silent for an awe,

stars in the firmament above him beaming,
　　stars in the firmament, alive and free,
stars, and of stars the innumerable streaming,
　　deep in the deeps, a river in the sea;—

these as he watched thro' march of their arising,
　　many in multitudes and one by one,
somewhat from God with a superb surprising
　　breathed in his eyes the promise of the sun.

So tho' our Daystar from our sight be taken,

   gone from his brethren, hidden from his own,

yet in his setting are we not forsaken,

   suffer not shadows of the dark alone.

Not in the west is Thine appearance ended,

   neither from night shall Thy renewal be,

lo, for the firmament in spaces splendid

   lighteth her beacon-fires ablaze for Thee :

holds them and hides and drowns them and discovers,

   throngs them together, kindles them afar,

showeth, o Love, Thy multitude of lovers,

   souls that shall know Thee and the saints that are.

Look what a company of constellations!

   Say can the sky so many lights contain?

Hath the great earth these endless generations?

   Are there so many purified thro' pain?

These thro' all glow and eminence of glory
    cry for a brighter, who delayeth long;
star unto star the everlasting story
    peals in a mystic sanctity of song.

Witness the hour when many saints assembled
    waited the Spirit, and the Spirit came;
ay with hearts tremulous and house that trembled,
    ay with cleft tongues, and the Holy Ghost, and flame.

Witness the men whom with a word He gaineth,
    bold who were base and voiceful who were dumb:—
Battle, I know, so long as life remaineth,
    battle for all, but these have overcome.

Witness the women, of His children sweetest,—
    scarcely earth seeth them but earth *shall* see,—
Thou in their woe Thine agony completest,
    Christ, and their solitude is nigh to Thee.

What is this psalm from pitiable places
 glad where the messengers of peace have trod?
Whose are these beautiful and holy faces
 lit with their loving and aflame with God?

Eager and faint, empassionate and lonely,
 these in their hour shall prophesy again:
this is His will who hath endured, and only
 sendeth the promise where He sends the pain.

Ay unto these distributeth the Giver
 sorrow and sanctity, and loves them well,
grants them a power and passion to deliver
 hearts from the prison-house and souls from hell.

Thinking hereof I wot not if the portal
 opeth already to my Lord above:
lo there is no more mortal and immortal,
 nought is on earth or in the heavens but love.

Hark what a sound, and too divine for hearing,
    stirs on the earth and trembles in the air!
Is it the thunder of the Lord's appearing?
    is it the music of His people's prayer?

Surely He cometh, and a thousand voices
    shout to the saints and to the deaf are dumb;
surely He cometh, and the earth rejoices
    glad in His coming who hath sworn, I come.

This hath He done and shall we not adore Him?
    this shall He do and can we still despair?
Come let us quickly fling ourselves before Him,
    cast at his feet the burthen of our care,

flash from our eyes the glow of our thanksgiving,
    glad and regretful, confident and calm,
then thro' all life and what is after living
    thrill to the tireless music of a psalm.

Yea thro' life, death, thro' sorrow and thro' sinning

He shall suffice me, for He hath sufficed:

Christ is the end, for Christ was the beginning,

Christ the beginning, for the end is Christ.

Cambridge:

PRINTED BY C. J. CLAY, M.A.
AT THE UNIVERSITY PRESS.